The new volume II of *Wedding Sermons and Marriage Ceremonies*, written by Derl Keefer, provides scriptural foundations for marriage expressed in relevant and fresh insights. Pastors will find this volume helpful as they prepare couples for marriage. The Biblical perspective is refreshing in a counterculture society that has dimensioned the value of marriage and home.

I would recommend this volume highly to pastors and marriage counselors.

Rev. Kevin C. Donley
Wisconsin District Superintendent
Church of the Nazarene

"*Wedding Sermons And Marriage Ceremonies Vol. 2* offers one of the most practical tools a pastor might have at his/her disposal. Whether it is a couple blending a family, seeking to renew vows, or any variation in-between, the Scriptural and well thought out ceremony elements provide a never-ending resource to established and new pastors alike. It will be my "go-to" resource in wedding planning for years to come."

Pastor Richard B. Doering, Racine Community Church of the Nazarene

I thought the content of Dr. Hartman's sermon was great. The wedding material was also great. Here is my endorsement. "It's always a big win for God's kingdom when seasoned pastor's share their wealth of experience with us. Pastoral Wedding Resources can save you a lot of time. It's well written and user friendly. Every pastor should have this in his arsenal."

Rev. Paul Booko
Riverside Church
Three Rivers, Michigan

In 32 years of pastoral ministry, I was always looking for resources for special events. Keefer and Hartman have written a much needed wedding resource for your library. Finding good resources for weddings was always a difficult thing to do, these two men have included resources that will enlighten the wedding experience and keep God in the center of the ceremony.

W. Glen Gardner,
District Superintendent
Eastern Michigan District
Myers-Briggs: ENFJ

Rev. Keefer offers the busy pastor a useful resource of fresh words and thoughts needed so that each bride and groom feel they are hearing something new. Rev. Keefer's writing through the years with sermon helps and outlines, devotional materials and other pastoral material provide a fundamental spiritually centered word for today. I recommend his new resource heartily to pastors.

Rev. Dr. Ronald L. Phelps, Pastor
Westlake Presbyterian Church
Bethany, Oklahoma

The wedding ceremony is sacred and Derl Keefer has laced these ceremonies with God's Word. His ceremonies are simple in beauty and very participatory as people become engaged in the wedding service. This is a great tool for pastors to use combining traditional liturgy with current style and procedure. Pastors can use them as a stand-alone ceremony or mix a bit of their own style with the service. Randy Hartman's homilies are user friendly by helping the pastor catch the flavor of ministry to the couple and their family and friends with his sermons.

Dr. Jim Dillow
Retired Pastor and District Superintendent
Joplin, Missouri District Church of the Nazarene

Derl Keefer and Randy Hartman have a written a book that has beautiful wedding ceremony ideas to fit a variety of marriage scenarios. A very useful tool for a pastor's toolkit.

Elena Meadows
Former Managing Editor
Commercial News
Three Rivers, Michigan

As a pastor, I'm always on the lookout for new and fresh ideas and materials for my ministry and personal development. This is true in every area of my ministry including places that can easily become predictable, plodding, and ritual. This is especially true in the marriage ceremonies that pastors have to develop. Many books on this subject tend to be carbon copies of one another and offer few new insights and fresh material. That is why I like the *Wedding Ceremonies and Sermons* book by Rev. Derl Keefer and Dr. Randall Hartman. I was able to glean new and fresh suggestions from this book to add new life to the wedding ceremonies I perform. I found their ideas practical, helpful, contemporary, and wonderfully different from similar books. I recommend this book wholeheartedly to the minister looking for new and fresh ideas for performing weddings!

Michael C. Wilson, Pastor
Word Fellowship Church
Centreville, Mi

Many pastors have plenty of resources for leadership and preaching, but for weddings, not so much. Rev. Keefer and Rev. Hartman have provided another great tool for this important ministry. The ceremonies provided are each distinct and follow a coherent theme. This is a great resource to help bring some freshness, creativity, and variety to the weddings you officiate.

Rev. Wilson Deaton
Lead Pastor
Church of the Nazarene
Kenosha, Wisconsin

Many ministerial students complete their college and seminary course work with little or no training in the preparation of wedding liturgy. For them, they usually take the easy route and use a denominational resource until such time that someone — often a spouse — suggests that they be more creative and write their own. In this excellent publication an experienced pastor has done the preliminary work to offer ministers alternatives to standard, traditional ceremonies. A minister can use these ideas as printed, or utilize them as "starters" for their own preparation. Couples will enjoy the finished product, as will families and friends who witness the wedding. I wish this resource had been available to me when I entered the ministry.

Dr. Tom Barnard
Former professor at Southern Nazarene University and Vice-president of Eastern Nazarene College in Wollaston, Massachusetts. He is an author and currently writes devotionals online.

I read the latest book from Derl Keefer and I highly recommend it to you. For busy pastors, there is often that feeling of being stuck. How can I say something new and creative and yet be true to Scripture and tradition? This book is a helpful for companion. At the minimum, this book will give you a new take and help to jump start your creativity. I highly recommend this book!

Dr. Ron Blake, former pastor and now District Superintendent for the Indianapolis District Church of the Nazarene. Dr. Blake was also Director of Ministerial Development at the General Headquarters of the Church of the Nazarene (now known as Global Ministry Center Church of the Nazarene).

Derl Keefer and Randy Hartman have compiled wedding sermons and marriage ceremonies that are fresh and relevant. Their insights and material will assist any pastor or wedding official looking for something to jumpstart their ideas or give a plan of action. This book is designed to be used and to use it is a must!

Dr. Ted Lee
Retired Pastor, Church Administrator and District Superintendent Church of the Nazarene

Maximizing pastors are always replenishing their ministry tool boxes with fresh ideas -- their own and those that emerge from the creative minds of other practitioners. With *Wedding Sermons and Marriage Ceremonies*, Keefer and Hartman rescue us from the well-worn rut of traditional ceremonies that may have outlived their usefulness. Their work is theologically sound, culturally relevant, and easily adaptable. Since our courts have attempted to redefine marriage, wedding officiants could adopt or adapt these sermons/ceremonies to remind everyone that, according to God's Word, marriage is a sacred covenantal relationship between a man and a woman. I recommend *Wedding Sermons and Marriage Ceremonies* to all who have the joyful privilege of solemnizing such unions.

Dr. Randy Berkner
Retired Superintendent,
North Arkansas District Church of the Nazarene
Author, Quantum Ministry: How Pastors Can Make the Leap

"Derl Keefer provides a life time of ministry experience in this practical and helpful marriage resource. The contents include 12 "themed" ceremonies, complete with Scripture readings, music suggestions, unique vows, and lots more.

This guide provides all a pastor needs in order to conduct thoughtful, meaningful marriage ceremonies."

Dr. Stan Reeder,
District Superintendent Church of the Nazarene Oregon/Pacific District

As a pastor of a small rural church, I don't officiate or attend many weddings; when I do, the ceremony planning is largely my responsibility. *Wedding Sermon and Marriage Ceremonies* will provide a rich resource to help me plan a meaningful and memorable ceremony in the midst of the small church pastoral life!

Mark Quinn
Nazarene Pastor

This book is a gift to the busy pastor. These thoughtful, helpful, and meaningful ceremonies reflect a lifetime of experience, and an awareness of current cultural realities. As someone who has been in the position of trying to find the right words for a wedding, this is a book I would keep close at hand. I look forward to gifting this to the pastors I know.

Janel Apps Ramsey
Evensong Community Church
Denver, Colorado

A well-executed wedding ceremony has the power to captivate the hearts and minds of everyone who participates. In this resource Rev. Keefer has provided a large selection of contemporary marriage ceremonies that can help pastors reach that objective.

Rev. Larry R. Morris, M.Div, MRE
Church of the Nazarene Global Ministry Center
Lenexa, Kansas

Wedding Sermons And Marriage Ceremonies

Volume 2

Derl Keefer
and
Randall Hartman

CSS Publishing Company, Inc.,
Lima, Ohio

WEDDING SERMONS AND MARRIAGE CEREMONIES
VOLUME 2

Copyright © 2019
CSS Publishing Company, Inc.
Lima, Ohio

The original purchaser may print and photocopy material in this publication for use as it was intended (worship material for worship use; educational material for classroom use; dramatic material for staging or production). No additional permission is required from the publisher for such copying by the original purchaser only. Inquiries should be addressed to: Permissions, CSS Publishing Company, Inc., 5450 N. Dixie Highway, Lima, Ohio 45807.

Scripture quotations marked (NIV) are taken from the Holy Bible, New International Version®, NIV®. Copyright © 1973, 1978, 1984, 2011 by Biblica, Inc.™ Used by permission of Zondervan. All rights reserved worldwide. www.zondervan.com. The "NIV" and "New International Version" are trademarks registered in the United States Patent and Trademark Office by Biblica, Inc.™

Scripture quotations marked (KJV) are from the King James Version of the Bible, in the public domain.

Scripture quotations marked CSB®, are taken from the Christian Standard Bible®, Copyright © 2017 by Holman Bible Publishers. Used by permission. Christian Standard Bible®, and CSB® are federally registered trademarks of Holman Bible Publishers.

Scripture quotations marked "The Message" are taken from The Message by Eugene H. Peterson, copyright © 1993, 1994, 1995, 1996, 2000, 2001, 2002. Used by permission of NavPress Publishing Group. All rights reserved.

e-book:
ISBN-13: 978-0-7880-2907-3
ISBN-10: 0-7880-2907-X

ISBN-13: 978-0-7880-
ISBN-10: 0-7880-2906-1

Digitally Printed

*To the light of my life, Karen,
who has been my true love, inspiration,
companion and wife for half a century!
You have my complete love!*
– Derl Keefer

*To my grown children,
Matthew and Emily,
who are the joy of my life and
the result of my own happy marriage!*
– Randal Hartman

Contents

Weddings — Prelude to Marriage   7

Marriage Ceremonies by Derl Keefer

Ceremony 1   11
God's Law of Love

Ceremony 2   15
Establishing A Lifetime of Value

Ceremony 3   19
Establishing a Christian Home

Ceremony 4   23
A Strong Family Marriage

Ceremony 5   27
Marriage — A Festival of Love

Ceremony 6   31
A Valentine Wedding

Ceremony 7   37
Prescription for a Successful Marriage

Ceremony 8   45
Marriage is More than a Dream — It is Love

Ceremony 9   49
God: The Foundation of Marriage

Ceremony 10   55
Gift of Love

Ceremony 11   59
Love Again

Ceremony 12   63
Renewing the Vows of Love

MUSIC SUGGESTIONS FOR WEDDINGS	67

Processionals
Vocals Or Instrumentals
Recessionals

SUGGESTED SCRIPTURES	69

Wedding Sermons by Randall Hartman

| Love's Got You Covered
1 Peter 4:8-11a	73
Looking Good!
Matthew 6:21-23	75
No Plan B
John 15:12-13	77
Getting Off On The Right Start
Joshua 24:14-15	79
Better Together
Genesis. 2:18-25	81
Dress For Marriage Success
Colossians 3:14-17	85
Off On An Adventure
Song of Songs 2:8-13	87
A New Land Awaits!
Deuteronomy 11:10-15	89
The Magical Power Of Love
1 Corinthians 13:4-7	91
One Plus One Equals One
Matthew 19:4-6	93
The Surprising Synergy Of Marriage
Ecclesiastes 4:9-10	95
The Way It Works
Ephesians 5:22-28	97

Weddings — Prelude to Marriage

There is a new house under construction in a subdivision I travel past. I have watched it being built. The foundation was dug and tons of dirt were excavated. Concrete, building timbers and other construction materials were place in just the right mixture to form a house. It is a work in progress. The home is going to be beautiful.

Just like that home, building strong marriages takes a ton of work! It will be a work in progress for a lifetime and will take of lot of building materials to make it strong and beautiful.

A minister is responsible by helping the couple to build their upcoming marriage through pre-marriage counseling. During this process questions will be asked, ideas will be floated, support will be given, and prayer will ascend to heaven as the couple begins their new venture together. The wedding ceremony will become the final plank in that process of pre-marriage counseling.

The wedding ceremony is a public occasion to celebrate the joining together of the lives of two individuals for a lifetime. A wedding should be viewed as both a religious and a social event. The ceremony will be the public pronouncement of the covenant the couple is making with each other and with God. It is social by its very nature of inviting others to join in the celebration of two lives becoming one. Celebration should be at the very core of the wedding.

The desire of Rev. Derl Keefer is to assist you by providing ceremonies that you can use in totality or supply ideas in creating your own ceremonies. Dr. Randall Hartman has provided homilies bringing Biblical emphasis into the ceremony. By marrying the homily and the ceremony together it will provide you with a great resource.

The following are suggestions as you work with the ceremonies:

1. Never be afraid to ask the couple what they would like to include in the ceremony.
2. Help the couple to enjoy the creativity of planning their own wedding ceremony.
3. Suggest they involve as many of their friends and family as possible in the ceremony.
4. Discover who will be in charge of the rehearsal and wedding day events. Do they have a wedding planner, or will you, or a parent, or someone from the family be the one in charge.
5. As the minister, you have a responsibility to make this a spiritual event in the lives of the couple and the congregation who have gathered for this occasion.
6. If an unforeseen circumstance arises meet it head on. Do not panic, but think it through and see it to its conclusion for example. As an example if it is an outdoor wedding and it rains, what is Plan B?
7. Rehearse the ceremony before you actually officiate at the service. Refresh your memory of the details before the actual ceremony.

Remember that God wants to bless this beautiful wedding day with His Divine Presence. Don't fail to ask Him to attend!
Derl G. Keefer

Marriage Ceremonies

by Derl Keefer

CEREMONY 1
God's Law of Love

Processional: "Traumerei" by Robert Schumann

Pastor: (Groom) and **(Bride)** you are being married under the laws of the land of this nation. Today you are also being married under the laws of God's authority.

God has set these laws for your marriage so that it will be successful and blessed throughout your lives. They are given for your protection, health, and spiritual maturity. As you apply God's commands, you will find true freedom in each other's hearts. Throughout this ceremony you will pledge yourselves to each other under the umbrella of God's redemptive covenant of laws.

As we begin this covenant, I ask who is it that gives this woman to be married to this man?

Father: Her family lovingly shares **(Bride)** with **(Groom)** with hope, joy and expectation for a happy life.

Pastor: (Groom) and (Bride), allow the lines of communication to be always open with each other. Paul counseled that conversations should always be full of grace by speaking the truth in love, sprinkled with compassion and mercy.

Groom: I, **(Groom)**, promise before you, this company and God that I will be faithful in sharing my heart and mind with you. My desire is to be an open book to you.

Bride: I, **(Bride)**, promise to be open in my communication with you as well. I will speak my mind and heart in love, compassion and mercy.

Pastor: Marriage is also a partnership. It is two hearts cooperating together under the leadership of the Holy Spirit. Your relationship is a cooperative effort to make satisfactory decisions that both of you can agree upon. It will save ill feelings and lessen the sting of arguments as well as honor Christ. The Bible tells us to make every effort to live in peace and harmony.

Bride and Groom (in unison): We will do our best to compromise and live in harmony as equal partners of faith in this marriage.

Pastor: Marriage is a celebration of two separate and unique individuals coming together by bringing their different gifts, abilities, values and strengths, galvanized and utilized by the power of God. **(Groom) and (Bride)** each of you have demonstrated that you recognize your differences and now celebrate in joy the bonding you will have throughout your life!

Special Music: "Come Live your Life With Me" Music by Nino Rota, Words by Larry Kusik and Billy Meshel

Let us ask God to bless this marriage today. **(Pastor prays).**

Pastor: (Groom) and (Bride) have vows they will now share with each other.

Groom: I love you **(Bride)** with all of my heart. As your husband I pledge to you that I will consider your needs first. I will keep affection and care of you as my highest priority. You will have my respect in all matters and I will never be too busy to be polite towards you. When necessary I will say "I am sorry" with meaning. You will continue to be my best friend. I will speak words of encouragement to you and be a positive influence in your life.

Bride: (Groom), you are the love and light of my life. I pledge my heart to you and my affection. You will always be my respected husband for life and I will show you my heart always. When necessary, I, too, will say "I am sorry" with meaning. You will continue to be my best friend. I will speak words to encourage you along life's journey and will be a positive influence in your life.

Pastor: (Groom) and (Bride) have rings that are symbols of their never-ending pledge of steadfast love. These rings are a circle that represents endless love.

Pastor's Blessing of the rings: May the rings you give today be a constant reminder of the endless love you pledge to one another and that God Himself blesses.

Groom (places ring on bride's finger): I give this ring with a never ending love.

Bride: I accept this ring of endless promise from you today and will wear it for life.

Bride (places ring on groom's finger): I give you this ring with a never ending love.

Groom: I accept this ring of endless promise from you today and will wear it for life.

Pastoral Prayer of Thanksgiving

Pastor: (Groom) and (Bride), as you have pledged your love and given rings as a sign of your relationship for life, I now pronounce you husband and wife. May the God of marriage bless and keep you forever.

Pastor: It is my honor to be the first to introduce to this congregation Mr. and Mrs. **(First Name)** and **(First Name) (Last Name).** What God has joined together, let nothing separate.

Recessional: "Romeo and Juliet Theme" by Tschaikowsky

CEREMONY 2
Establishing A Lifetime of Value

Processional: Bridal Chorus "Lohengrin" by Wagner

Pastor: Dear Friends: **(Groom) and (Bride)** have decided to establish a marriage and a home based on the intrinsic value of God's desire for life partnership. Their individual and corporate values will influence the decisions, words, and actions in their lives, their marriage and the home they are establishing today. Why are these values important? It is because they will guide them in decision making, impact the way they treat each other, influence their overall behavior and communicate their priorities. This couple has discovered their value system is based on God's Holy Word and the Savior, Jesus Christ, whom they have invited into their lives and marriage. Their values will help them walk worthily in their lives in holiness, light and love.

Paul urges this value system when he writes to the Ephesians: "I urge you to live a life worthy of the calling you have received. Be completely humble and gentle; be patient, bearing with one another in love. Make every effort to keep the unity of the Spirit through the bond of peace. There is one body and one Spirit, just as you were called to one hope when you were called; one Lord, one faith, one baptism; one God and Father of all who is over all and through all and in all. But to each one of us grace has been given…" (Ephesians 4:1b-7a NIV).

Pastor: (Groom) and (Bride), starting a relationship began some time ago for you and has matured and developed into full blown love! Today we have gathered in this place to witness your pledges of love in a lifelong commitment. How amazing is God's grace to give you His blessing.

Groom: (Bride), I bring into this marriage relationship a different background, history, family and personality, but I see how in the context of our love this will bring adventure and excitement to our relationship. My hope and dream is that this new relationship will affect you in positive and motivating ways for our lifetime together. **(Bride)**, I love you!

Bride: (Groom), I, too, am bringing into this marriage relationship my own background, history, family and personality. I envision it to be a marriage of adventure and excitement that the two of us will share together. I accept your hope and dream of our lives together being a lifetime filled with motivation and positive fulfillment for our love. **(Groom)**, I love you!

Special Song: "I Come to Thee" by Beatrice Fenner and Adapted by Chester Nordman

Pastor: Friends of **(Groom) and (Bride)**, I have observed through my time of counseling with this couple that they sincerely want this marriage to be a wholesome arena of happiness and joy, where friends and neighbors can observe the transparency that is in both of them. Though there will always be times of imperfections and moments of frustrations and disagreements, I believe they will work together to make life the best possible for each other.

Please face one another as you exchange vows.

Groom: (Bride), I give you my heart and love. I covenant to you that I will do my best to be patient, kind, forgiving, honest and loving always. You have made my heart leap with joy and I give you my life forever. I invite God into our marriage to bless and guide.

Bride: (Groom), I give you my heart and love. I covenant to you that I will do my best to be patient, kind, forgiving, honest and loving always. You have made my heart leap with joy and I give you my life forever. I invite God into our marriage to bless and guide.

Pastor: What sign do you give as a pledge of your unending love?

Bride/Groom: A ring.

Groom: (Bride), I give you this ring as a pledge of my unending love for you.

Bride: (Groom), I accept this ring from you.

Bride: (Groom), I give you this ring as a pledge of my unending love for you.

Groom: (Bride), I accept this ring from you.

Pastor: (Groom) and (Bride) have asked to light a unity candle commemorating this time of solemn vows and sharing their future together.

(Couple lights the unity candle as the song "You Light Up My Life" is played).

Pastor (as couple returns to places): Friends, since **(Groom) and (Bride)** have given rings as a pledge of their love and faithfulness I, **(Pastor)**, pronounce them husband and wife. What God has joined together, let no one separate.

Pastor: (Groom), you may now kiss your bride!

Pastor: Family and friends, let me be the first to introduce to you Mr. and Mrs. **(Grooms First and Last Name).**

Recessional: "Wedding March" by Mendelssohn

CEREMONY 3
Establishing a Christian Home

Any couple can establish a home, but you are specifically desiring to establish a Christian home. Today as you declare before this company of people including family and friends from both of your lives, you are sharing your faith in Christ. Your declaration includes honor to the Trinity, the Word of God as the Bible describes, and the character of God.

The foundations of a Christian home are important. Today you will be expressing your commitment to it through declarations, pronouncements, exchange of rings, communion, lighting a unity candle and more.

Groom: (Bride) and I want to begin our married lives following the Scripture's admonishment to *"Seek first his kingdom and his righteousness…"* Matthew 6:33. As we do we firmly believe that our lives will be a blessing to Him, to others and to one another.

Bride: (Groom) and I want to *"Be imitators of God, therefore, as dearly loved children and live a life of love, just as Christ loved us and gave himself up for us as a fragrant offering and sacrifice to God"* as Paul wrote to the Ephesians in 5:1.

Pastor: Establishing a Christian home takes courage, understanding, love and dedication from both of you. It is not a one sided experience. It is learning how to love as Christ loved you.

Groom: (Bride), my heart's desire is to give you all that you need… compassion, understanding, hope, friendship and God's love.

Bride: (Groom) my heart's desire is to give you all that you need… compassion, understanding, hope, friendship and God's love.

Bride and Groom: Today, we make a commitment to a lifelong experience that will draw us together in a marriage relationship that will last throughout our lives.

Pastor: Perhaps the greatest blessing in marriage is that it lasts so long. The years will produce a deepening of interest in each other. If it were short term it would be like a series of temporary relationships where you miss the ripening, gathering, harvesting of joys that are deep and hard won truths of marriage.

Special Music: "Come Live your Life With Me" Music by Nino Rota and Words by Larry Kusik and Billy Meshel

Pastor: (Groom) and (Bride) have asked that communion be given to them and all who are here today. Communion is a celebration of the life and death of Jesus with a hope of salvation that is given to all believers. If you would like to participate in communion, the ushers will be passing the elements to you.

(After all have been served, the pastor should use the communion service liturgy specific to their theological position.)

Exchange of Rings

Pastor: The circle of this ring symbolizes the never-ending trust you have in one another.

Pastor to Groom: (Groom), place this ring on **(Bride's)** finger and repeat after me.

Pastor: I, **(Groom)**, take you, **(Bride)**, to be my treasured wife for the rest of my life.

Bride: I accept this ring with my trust in you.

Pastor to Bride: (Bride), place this ring on **(Groom's)** finger and repeat after me.

Pastor: I, **(Bride)**, take you, **(Groom)**, to be my treasured husband for the rest of my life.

Groom: I accept this ring with my trust in you.

Pastor: (Groom) and **(Bride)** have requested to light a unity candle signifying their desire to be one in heart.

Lighting of the Unity Candle by the Couple
(as a reading from *Sonnets From The Portuguese* by Elizabeth Barrett Browning is read):

Instrumental Music: "You Light Up My Life"

Pastor: (To Congregation): I ask of you to lend your hearts, prayers and concerns to this couple now and always. If so say, "Yes, we will."

Congregation: Yes, we will.

Pastor: (To Couple): Since you **(Groom)** and **(Bride)** have exchanged vows and rings with one another before this congregation of witnesses, I pronounce you husband and wife by the authority of the (Church) and the state of (State). God has joined you together; let nothing separate you from each other or from Him. **(Groom)** you may now kiss your bride!

Pastor: (To Congregation): Ladies and Gentlemen, it is my distinct pleasure to be the first to introduce you to Mr. and Mrs. **(Grooms First and Last Name)**.

Recessional: "Wedding March" by Mendelssohn

CEREMONY 4

A Strong Family Marriage

(This ceremony is for a second marriage with children)

Pastor: Today, **(Groom) and (Bride)** have asked you as their family and friends to gather with them to celebrate their marriage. They have requested that their children be involved in this important ceremony where they will pledge publicly their vows to each other.

Together they have discovered that their individual love has found a home in purpose and fulfillment, and it is in each other. Desiring to cultivate the conditions of that love and to fulfill its highest meaning, they want to pass that along to their children (name of children can be inserted here).

Pastor (To children): Your parents have had some obstacles along their life's journey, but have found love for each other and a love for you as well. They want to you to know that they believe God has given them this love and with his divine purpose has brought them together. They are marrying because they want to experience God's best for their lives and for yours.

Pastor (To Congregation): We come as family and friends to celebrate with **(Groom) and (Bride)** this glowing love filled with happiness and joy for this wonderful occasion.

Pastoral Prayer: Dear Father, we come into your Holy Presence requesting a special blessing upon **(Groom) and (Bride)** and upon their family. Join them in this new destiny throughout their lives. Today they give verbal vows and listen to each other's heart. Help them to know that every moment will be centered on each other and as they combine families -- upon their new family as well. It comes only as all hearts reach for you and your example of love. May their hearts have the glow of joy and happiness now and throughout their lives. We ask this in Your Son's name. Amen.

Soloist: "Grow Old with Me" by John Lennon.

Pastor (To Groom): Do you, **(Groom)**, take **(Bride)** to be your wife as you begin this journey of marriage? Do you promise to give her your complete attention? Will you often express your love to her? Do you covenant to be devoted to her in all of life's matters? Will your relationship be honest and trustworthy with her? If so say, "I do."

Groom: I do.

Pastor (To Bride): Do you, **(Bride)**, take **(Groom)** to be your husband as you begin this journey of marriage? Do you promise to give him your complete attention? Will you often express your love to him? Do you covenant to be devoted to her in all of life's matters? Will your relationship be honest and trustworthy with him? If so say, "I do."

Bride: I do

CHILDREN OR FRIENDS OF THE COUPLE WILL READ ADAPTED PORTIONS OF I CORINTHIANS 13

> **Reader 1:** Love is patient and kind, Love is not jealous.
> **Reader 2:** Love is not conceited, or proud, or provoked.
> **Reader 3:** Love does not keep a record of wrong doings.
>
> **Reader 1:** Love is not happy with evil, harshness or conceit.
> **Reader 2:** Love is pleased when the truth is told.
> **Reader 3:** Love never gives up on people;

All Readers in Unison: Love brings faith, hope and patience in one another.

RING CEREMONY

Pastor: Do you, **(Groom) and (Bride)**, have rings to share with one another?

Couple: Yes, we do.

(Pastor receives rings from the Best Man and Maid of Honor)

Pastor (Holding up the rings so that all can see them): The circle of these rings symbolizes the enduring trust, hope and love that these two have for each other.

Pastor (to Groom who places ring on Bride's finger): I, **(Groom)**, give you this ring in solemn covenant taking you as my wife as a gift from Almighty God, and I will treasure you for the remainder of my life.

Pastor (to Bride who places ring on Groom's finger): I, **(Bride)**, give you this ring in solemn covenant taking you as my husband as a gift from Almighty God and I will treasure you for the remainder of my life.

Solo: "With This Ring" by Clyde Otis and Vincent Corso, Hudson Bay Music, Inc.

Prayer of Thanksgiving is given by one of the children or close friend of the couple.

Pastor: Bringing a blended family together is not an easy task, but with the support of each other, the cooperation of children, and prayers from family and friends, it is attainable. You are starting life together right... you are beginning it with God's undergirding help. Keep relying on Him... Keep your focus on Christ... Let the difficult moments be worked out together and let no one or anything come between the two of you and your love.

Pastor: Since you have exchanged vows and rings with each other before this congregation of friends and family, I pronounce you husband and wife to live together until death parts you. **(Groom)**, you may now kiss your bride.

Pastor: (Groom) and (Bride), please turn and face the congregation. Ladies and gentlemen, let me be the first to introduce to you, Mr. and Mrs. **(Groom First and Last Name)**.

Recessional: "How Firm a Foundation" Early American

CEREMONY 5
Marriage — A Festival of Love

Processional: Entrance of the wedding party to the music of "Hail Thee, Festival Day" by Ralph Vaughan Williams, 1872-1958

Pastor: We gather today to celebrate true love that culminates in marriage between two people who have discovered the understanding of love. **(Groom)** and **(Bride)** have seen what meaning there is in life as they face it together. This celebration of love may be a brief ceremony, but every day they live the affirmations and declarations that they are making today will be treasured. We rejoice with these two people who found each other from all others in the world and who will pledge to commit themselves before these witnesses today. Each come into this ceremony as unique individuals, but will also celebrate their combined faith and hope in God.

Giving Away of the Bride by parents

Pastor: Who gives this woman to be married to this man?

Parents: We, her parents on behalf of her family, share her with **(Groom)**.

Reading: 1 Corinthians 13:4-8, 13(NIV)

> "*Love is patient, love is kind. It does not envy, it does not boast, it is not proud. It does not dishonor others, it is not self-seeking, it is not easily angered, it keeps no record of wrongs. Love does not delight in evil but rejoices with the truth. It always protects, always trusts, always hopes,*

always perseveres. Love never fails. But where there are prophecies, they will cease; where there are tongues, they will be stilled; where there is knowledge, it will pass away... And now these three remain: faith, hope and love. But the greatest of these is love."

Reading: Matthew 5:13-16

"You are the salt of the earth. But if the salt loses its saltiness, how can it be made salty again? It is no longer good for anything, except to be thrown out and trampled underfoot.

You are the light of the world. A town built on a hill cannot be hidden. Neither do people light a lamp and put it under a bowl. Instead they put it on its stand, and it gives light to everyone in the house. In the same way, let your light shine before others, that they may see your good deeds and glorify your Father in heaven."

The Story of the Couple

Pastor: (Groom) and (Bride) have written the story of how they met and how they fell in love. The bride's mother is reading this on their behalf.

Song: "Come, Ye Blessed" Words: Matthew 25:34-36/ Music by John Prindle Scott, 1877-1932

Homily by the Pastor

Song: "How Great Thou Art" Words by Carl Boberg, 1859-1940/Music is a Swedish folk melody.

Exchange of Vows and Rings

Pastor: You have been brought together in a wonderful way of love. It it time you now pledge to honor this gift of His love by making your vows to each other.

Pastor: (Groom), please make this vow to your bride.

Groom: Before God and these witnesses, I, **(Groom)**, take you **(Bride)**, to be the one who complements my life in this world. I pledge my faithfulness to you. I will be with you in the good times and in the difficult times. I will believe in you and affirm you at every opportunity. You can feel free to lean on my shoulder anytime you want and I will care for you always!

Bride: Before God and these witnesses, I, **(Bride)**, take you **(Groom)**, to be the one that complements my life in this world. I pledge my faithfulness to you. I will be with you in the good times and in the difficult times. I will believe in you and affirm you at every opportunity. You can feel free to lean on my shoulder anytime you want and I will care for you always!

Pastor: The wedding ring is a symbol of valuable promises. The Old Testament people had seals that were fixed on letters or important documents to guarantee that it was genuine and personal. It was a visible mark. These wedding rings are the symbols of your commitment. It is a visible symbol to all the world of your importance to one another.

Please place the wedding ring on the ring finger and repeat after me:

Groom: This ring I give to you as my promise of love and faithfulness throughout our lives.

Bride: This ring I give to you as my promise of love and faithfulness throughout our lives.

Pastor: (Groom) and (Bride), would you please turn and look at this congregation. Ladies and Gentlemen, it is my honor to introduce for the first time, Mr. and Mrs. **(Last Name)**.

Recessional: "Non Nobis, Domine" from Henry V Music: Patrick Doyle, b. 1953.

After the last of the wedding party has left and the music softens, the pastor walks to the center of the platform and says:

You have witnessed the marriage of **(Groom) and (Bride)**. They are in love, but there will be times in their marriage when they will need not only each other's love, but our love as well. They will need our counsel, our wisdom, our mentoring, and most importantly our prayers. My sincere request to all of you is that you give them those items freely as their friends or family.

Now, may the God of marriage go with each of you as you leave today. May His face shine upon you and His love overwhelm you… Now and Forevermore. In the Name of the Father, and of the Son and of the Holy Spirit.

Recessional: Wedding March ("Midsummer Night's Dream" by Mendelssohn)

CEREMONY 6
A Valentine Wedding

Processional: "O God of Love" by Niccum

Pastor: The Bible is filled with examples of lovers who become forever valentines. The first couple that the Scriptures note as valentine lovers is Adam and Eve. As the story goes God made Adam out of the dust of the ground, but realizes that Adam needed someone like him to share his thoughts, dreams and life.

God makes woman from the side of man. Adam says of her, "This is now bone of my bones and flesh of my flesh; she shall be called 'woman' for she was taken out of man." (Genesis 2:23 NIV). The writer of Genesis continues the narrative by commenting, "That is why a man leaves his father and mother and is united with his wife, and they become one flesh." (Genesis 2:24 NIV)

The second valentine lovers were Jacob and Rachel and their story is also told in the book of Genesis chapter 29 and beyond. Jacob had to leave his home because of a family feud and traveled a long ways finally arriving at Paddan Aram where he meets Rachel and her family. After staying with them for a period of time and working for his Uncle Laban he seeks the hand of Rachel. The Bible says, "Jacob was in love with Rachel." (Genesis 29:18 NIV) He commits himself to work for Laban for seven years in order to marry Rachel. The truth is that seven years became fourteen years, but he was committed to marrying Rachel. Why? Back to Genesis 29:18... he loved her!

Pastor: (Groom) and **(Bride)** love each other! They are valentines to one another and this marriage is the start of the celebration of love for the rest of their lives!

Pastor: Where does love begin? I believe that love is initiated by God. He demonstrates for us how to have that "forever" love that connects us to a hope in one another. He invests in us by encouraging us through experience, appreciation and maturity. So today, friends, you have come to witness the marriage of **(Groom) and (Bride)**. Their valentine love is in the hands of God.

Pastor (To the Father): Who gives this woman to be married to this man?

Father: Her family, who loves her, gives her to this man for a lifetime of commitment through God's covenant of love. (Father then kisses his daughter and places her hand in the groom's hand).

Pastor: If you want your life to be caressed with beauty, then remember the days of your courtship with cherished thoughts. Even through the routine of everyday living that all of us experience, refuse to allow the vision of marriage to be blurred.

A valentine heart is one that God gives through love, joy, hope and goodness as it is practiced on a daily basis. The best place for this to occur is in the home. Becoming a husband or a wife does not destroy your individuality. God helps us to enhance and enrich your natural skills, abilities and talents. Allow God to help you grow and develop as a loving couple. Work together to be at your best for one another by being intimate, open and fulfilling in your relationship.

As we pray, let us address our God for what He is… a loving and caring Father who gives us love!

Friend of the couple: Let us pray… (Extemporaneous or written prayer by a friend of either of the couple).

Pastor: What do you two have as a symbol of your love and commitment to one another?

Couple: We bring rings as our symbol of devotion, love and commitment. (best man and matron/maid of honor give rings to the pastor, who then hands to the couple).

Special Music: "With This Ring" (Words and Music by Clyde Otis and Vincent Corso, Hudson Bay Music, Inc.).

Pastor: These rings that have been handed to you are made of gold. They were refined in fire to make them pure and strong. Let them symbolize your purity and strength for your lives together.

Pastor: (To Groom) Place the ring on **(Bride's)** finger and repeat after me.

Pastor: (Groom Repeats) I, **(Groom)**, give you this ring, **(Bride)**, out of a love that never ends. I know this ring is only a symbol, but it is a forever symbol of my love and devotion to you.

Bride: I, **(Bride)**, receive this ring from you, **(Groom)**, as your symbol of love and devotion to me.

Pastor (To Bride): Place this ring on **(Groom's)** finger and repeat after me.

Pastor: (Bride Repeats) I, **(Bride)**, give you this ring, **(Groom)**, out of love that never ends. I know this ring is only a symbol, but it is a forever symbol of my love and devotion to you.

Groom: I, **(Groom)**, receive this ring from you, **(Bride)**, as your symbol of love and devotion to me.

Pastor: Today, **(Groom) and (Bride)** you have vows to share with one another to seal this marriage for a lifetime.

Special Music: "Because" by D'Hardelto

Groom: (Repeats vows or reads them or has them memorized): My wonderful bride, I love you as a forever valentine that God has placed in my heart. God's values are my values for you that include faith, hope and love. God's priorities are my priorities for our relationship that encompasses time we spend together, moments we share through good times and painful times, and the exploration of life all of our lives. God has given us a vision, goals to achieve, and dreams to accomplish together. I love you!

Bride: (Repeats vows or reads them or has them memorized): My wonderful husband, I love you as a forever valentine that God has placed in my heart. God's values are my values for you that include faith, hope and love. God's priorities are my priorities for our relationship that encompasses time we spend together, moments we share through good times and painful times, and the exploration of life for all of our lives. God has given us a vision, goals to achieve, and dreams to accomplish together. I love you!

Pastoral Prayer: Let's ask God's blessing on these two people who have shared rings and made vows together.

> *"God of love who expressed faithfulness and hope in the person of our Lord and Savior Jesus Christ, I ask Your holy blessing on the words that (Bride) and (Groom) have shared with one another. May these vows reflect not only a trust in each other, but also in You. Before every decision is made, may they seek Your guidance and direction. When adversity hits, may they quickly seek refuge in You. May they laugh*

often, may their joy bubble up from a spring of living water, and may they respond to each other when tears flow and allow their tears to fall upon your caring and loving heart. I pray that their vows be words of action on their life's journey together. Holy Spirit be their Guide! May they truly have valentine hearts of love. In your name we pray. Amen"

Pronouncement by Pastor
The celebration of this sacred and somber moment and the giving of vows and the exchanging of rings gives me the honor by the church and the state to pronounce the two loving hearts to be husband and wife.

Pastor: (To Groom) You may now kiss your bride.

Pastor: May I have the privilege to be the first to introduce you to Mr. and Mrs. **(Groom First and Last Name)**.

Recessional by the bridal party: "Trumpet Air" by Purcell. Pastor give the benediction to the congregation before his/her exit: The grace and love of our Lord Jesus Christ be with your spirit, brothers and sisters. Amen.

CEREMONY 7
Prescription for a Successful Marriage

Processional: "Panis Angelicus" by Franck (Ethel Smith Music Corp., Miami Beach, Fla, 1949).

Pastor: Dear Friends, The Biblical story about a builder who built his house upon the sand… they were built upon a weak foundation of dreams. Norman Wright wrote, "When we dream, our minds do not have to distinguish between reality or fantasy, so we create without restraint. Often therefore, our dreams are the starting points for successful endeavors; however, dreams that are not followed by adequate planning do not come true." Building a good, strong, vibrant marriage means that you two must take to define roles, beliefs, and behaviors and negotiate the differences with your partner. As you, **(Groom)** and **(Bride)** take your vows, exchange rings, and pledge yourselves to each other, you will find the prescription for a successful marriage that is built on a rock and not sand.

Pastor: To this end, do you **(Groom)** and **(Bride)**, commit your lives to one another in the sight of God and these witnesses who are your friends and family. If so, answer, "We do."

Couple: We do.

Pastor to Groom: Will you, **(Groom)**, take this woman to be your lawfully wedded wife? Will you live together under the leadership of God in the holy relationship of marriage? Will you pledge today to love her, honor her, comfort her, and keep her whether she is sick or healthy? Will you forsake all other relationships to keep yourself only to her as long as you both shall live? If so, respond, "I will."

Groom: I will.

Pastor to Bride: Will you, **(Bride)**, take this man to be your lawfully wedded husband? Will you live together under the leadership of God in the holy relationship of marriage? Will you pledge today to love him, honor him, comfort him, and keep him whether he is sick or healthy? Will you forsake all other relationships to keep yourself only to him as long as you both shall live? If so, respond, "I will."

Bride: I will.

Pastor to Parents: The blessing of the home being established today comes from homes that have had positive influences on these two individuals. Who gives this couple to each other?

Parents of the Groom: As his parents, we give him to this wonderful woman of his dreams.

Parents of the Bride: As her parents, we give her to this wonderful man of her dreams.

Scripture Reading by Best Man:

> *So chosen by God for this new life of love, dress in the wardrobe God picked out for you: compassion, kindness, humility, quiet strength, discipline. Be even-tempered, content with second place, quick to forgive an offense. Forgive as quickly and completely as the Master forgave you. And regardless of what else you put on, wear love. It's your basic, all-purpose garment. Never be without it."* (Colossians 3:12-14 Message Bible).

Scripture Reading by Maid or Matron of Honor:

"Let the peace of Christ keep you in tune with each other, in step with each other. None of this going off and doing your own thing. And cultivate thankfulness. Let the Word of Christ — the Message — have the run of the house. Give it plenty of room in your lives. Instruct and direct one another using good common sense...Let every detail in your lives — words, actions, whatever — be done in the name of the Master, Jesus, thanking God the Father every step of the way." (Colossians 3:15-17 Message Bible).

Pastor to Groom: (Groom), "Go all out in love for your wife. Never take advantage of her. Never let a day go by without telling her how much you love her. Never let the day end in anger, but go to bed with forgiveness and care in your heart."

Pastor to Bride: (Bride), always be understanding with your husband. Support him in his endeavors. Be his sounding board as decisions are made that affect your lives. Listen, give advice, show empathy and be his best friend for life.

Pastor to Couple: If you do this, your marriage will be enriched beyond words. In keeping with the instruction of the God's Word, let us make your vows to one another.

Pastor to Groom (Groom Repeats Vows): Before God, our parents, our family and friends, I, **(Groom)**, take you, **(Bride)**, to be my wife, to have and to hold starting this day in times of plenty and in times of need, in sickness and in health, to love with an enduring love, until death separates us.

Pastor to Bride (Bride Repeats Vows): Before God, our parents, our family and friends, I, **(Bride)**, take you, **(Groom)**, to be my husband, to have and to hold starting this day in times of plenty and in times of need, in sickness and in health, to love with an enduring love, until death separates us.

Pastor: The wedding rings you are giving to each other typify your marriage. The ring is round symbolizing your vows of allegiance that never end. The gold (or silver) symbolizes the strength that your pledge maintains to faithfulness. The placement on the finger tells the world that you are pledged to each other and let no one attempt to separate you.

Pastor to Groom: (Groom), what symbol do you have of your wedding vow?

Groom to Pastor: I have this ring to offer to my beloved.

Pastor to Groom: (Groom), place this ring on your bride's finger and repeat after me:

Groom to Bride: This ring I give to you, in pledge of my faithfulness to you and my abiding love.

Pastor to Bride: (Bride), what symbol do you have of your wedding vow?

Bride to Pastor: I have this ring to offer to my beloved.

Pastor to Bride: (Bride), place this ring on your groom's finger and repeat after me:

Bride to Groom: This ring I give to you, in pledge of my faithfulness to you and my abiding love.

Special Music: "I Love Thee" by Edvard Grieg

Pastor: God's Holy Word declares what true, honest to God love is and how it should be lived. Love's definition is discovered in 1 Corinthians 13:4-7. It will be read by the parents of the **Bride and Groom:**

Father of the Groom: Love is patient, love is kind. It does not envy, it does not boast, it is not proud.

Father of the Bride: It is not rude, it is not self-seeking, it is not easily angered, it keeps no record of wrongs.

Mother of the Groom: Love does not delight in evil but rejoices with the truth.

Mother of the Bride: Love always protects, always trusts, always hopes, always perseveres.

Candle Ceremony Signifying Unity in the Marriage

Pastor: (Groom) and **(Bride)**, as you continue making vows to one another, it is further accomplished through the symbol of the lighting of the unity candle. The three candles uniquely express what is happening today in your lives. The two outer candles remind us of your individuality, creating the beauty God has bestowed upon your lives as made in His spiritual image. The middle candle suggests that your lives are now merged together in a common focus on each other and upon God. As the flames are brought together of your separate candles let it represent the unity you have in heart, and in faith, in in life.

Communion Ceremony

Pastor: As a Christ-centered couple, **(Groom)** and **(Bride)** have requested communion be served to those who desire to participate. As I serve, **(Groom)** and **(Bride)** individually, I would remind you that the bread represents the Body of our Lord Jesus Christ and the cup of wine represents the blood of our Lord Jesus Christ. Let all who wish come to the Lord's table. There are places that are set up for you to go to and participate at those locations. You will be served by the wedding party. Once you have been served please return to your seats. You may go now at your discretion.

Music: "Largo" (Xerxes) by Handel

Once all have returned to their seats and the couple has been served, the pastor will continue with **Prayer:**

> *Almighty God who has shown us what love means through sacrifice and faithfulness, we ask your blessing on these hearts who establish their home on this day. We pray that they will seek You as the source of direction, wisdom, hope and strength. May your holy presence fill their lives with laughter, joy, peace, and faithfulness on their journey together. May they always sense your holy presence in the center of their lives. May your word be the centerpiece of learning about each other and may your Holy Spirit be their guide. May they honor You by being the Christians they profess to each other and to the world in which they live. As children come into this union, may they see the true meaning of love and commitment as demonstrated by their parents* **(Groom)** *and* **(Bride)**. *We praise Your name. Amen.*

Pastor: (Groom) and **(Bride)** have agreed to live together under the authority of God and have witnessed this before each of you. I pronounce them husband and wife, in the name of the Father, and the Son, and the Holy Spirit. Those whom God has joined together let no one separate.

Pastor to Groom: (Groom), you may now kiss your bride. Now, it is my honor to introduce for the very first time, Mr. and Mrs. **(Groom's First and Last Name).**

Bridal Party leaves and the pastor steps to the center of the platform and pronounces the Benediction.

Recessional: How Firm a Foundation

> *"May the grace of the Lord Jesus Christ, and the love of God, and the fellowship of the Holy Spirit be with you"* (2 Corinthians 13:14 NIV).

The audience is dismissed.

CEREMONY 8
Marriage is More than a Dream — It is Love

Processional: Jesus, Joy of Man's Desiring

Pastor: (Groom) and **(Bride)** Often we come into a marriage with a dream of what marriage should be. Love is the key component of that dream. Love is more than a dream… it is the reality of it all! Today as you take your vows and make commitments to each other you will express that dream of love.

Groom: (Bride) my true love I give you my invitation to begin our love story for a lifetime. It will include our acceptance of one another… our life together until the day we die… that we are completing a wholeness through our love and a happiness that will never end with one another.

Bride: (Groom) I accept your invitation of starting our love story together for a lifetime. I envision that the dream will become our reality and that we will tell our grandchildren how that love began and continued throughout our lives.

Pastor: There is always an excitement when we talk about our dreams, but there is always a reality as well. Companionship comes alive. How does that happen?

Groom: (Bride), I want our dreams to come alive by sharing my thoughts, ideas and hopes through my conversations with you. I have many friends, but there is no friend as close to my heart as you.

Bride: (Groom), I want to listen to your dreams as you will with mine. My desire is that both of us will share our conversations that bring alive those thoughts, ideas and hopes. You are my closest friend in my heart.

Groom: (Bride), let's embrace life to the fullest. When I am with you all the world is right! I love you!

Bride: (Groom), embracing life with you is going to be exhilarating and I am ready to explore the world with you. I love you!

Pastor: (Groom) and **(Bride)**, I charge you both to keep love at the center of your lives. Love means you are open with one another and that you enjoy one another's company more than anyone else's company. Love will give your lives opportunities to serve each other and to be of service to the world you live in today and for the future. Love will witness the growth of maturity.

The Bible declares in Hebrews that we are to honor marriage and be faithful to marriage, and remain faithful to one another in marriage.

Pastor: Your family and friends are gathered here today to witness this special occasion that celebrates a wedding, a marriage and love. As you pledge your love for each… do so in love.

Groom: (Bride), before God, our friends and family, I, **(Groom)**, take you, **(Bride)**, to be my true love forever. I pledge to you my complete faithfulness, respect, and love and I also pledge that no one will separate us.

Bride: (Groom), before God, our friends and family, I, **(Bride)**, take you, **(Groom)**, to be my true love forever. I pledge to you my complete faithfulness, respect and love and I also pledge that no one will separate us.

Pastor: Rings have been a symbol of marriages for years because of their symbolism of value. The circle of the ring is the symbol of unending allegiance of love for all of time. Please place the ring on the finger and repeat after me.

Groom: (Bride), with this ring I give you my promise of faithful love.

Bride: (Groom), I receive this ring with complete trust and faith in you.

Bride: (Groom), with this ring I give you my promise of faithful love.

Groom: (Bride), I receive this ring with complete trust and faith in you.

Scripture Reading

Pastor: Friends will read various Scriptures now.

> Reading 1: John 13:34-35 (Read from Message Bible)
> Reading 2: Proverbs 3:1-6 (Read from King James Version)
> Reading 3: Psalm 103:17-18 (Read from New International Version)
> Reading 4: I John 3:18a (Read from Holy Bible: Easy to Read Version)

Pastor to Groom: Repeat after me:

Pastor: I, **(Groom)**, take you, **(Bride)**, to be my wife in love and hope of our life together. I pledge to you my undying hope in our future.

Pastor to Bride: Repeat after me:

Pastor: I, **(Bride)**, take you, **(Groom)**, to be my hus-band in love and hope of our life together. I pledge to you my undying hope in our future.

Special Music

Pastor to Groom and Bride: **(Groom)** and **(Bride)**, it is now my joy, granted to me by the state of **(State)** and the **(Church)**, to declare to all that you are husband and wife. You have freely given commitments to one another. I charge you to become one in your relationship.

Pastor to Groom: You may now kiss your bride!

Pastor: It is my distinct pleasure to introduce you for the very first time, Mr. and Mrs. **(Groom's First and Last Name)**.
Wedding party leaves to the music of "Guide Me, O Thou Great Jehovah"

Pastor to Audience: This couple needs your complete support. Do not disappoint them, but build them up in faith, hope and love.

"May you go in love, hope and peace now and forever!"

CEREMONY 9
God: The Foundation of Marriage

Processional: "Love Theme" from Romeo and Juliet
The Genesis story of the Garden of Eden is a starting point for us to understand the foundation of marriage. The Genesis account relates to us that God has "made man out of the dust of the ground forming him into the shape He wanted and then God breathed into his nostrils the breath of life and man became a living being." (Genesis 2:7 NIV) God names him Adam. Adam had the whole garden and living space to use for himself. He had the open air and sky as his canopy for living and sleeping. He had places to fish (Genesis 2:10) along with a fantastic job (Genesis 2:15), lots to eat (Genesis 2:16), a whole area to walk paths (the entire Garden of Eden), and God to talk with everyday. All of this, but something was missing in Adam's life... human companionship -- someone to share a relationship with who would understand him on his level, a person to share his heart and soul with and walk alongside him in life's journey. Adam needed an Eve and God solved the problem and introduced Eve to Adam (Genesis 2:22). It truly was a match made in heaven!

Throughout the Holy Scriptures God gives us the thought of what a strong foundational marriage can be for those who desire it.

Pastor: (Groom) and **(Bride)** you are coming to-gether today to establish a strong marriage in the sight of God and before these witnesses two are family and friends. It means there are a lot of changes that will enter your lives in the future. One of those is leaving your parents' homes and establishing your own independent lives together.

Pastor: Who gives this woman to be married to this man?

Father of the Bride: Her father and mother who have loved her from her first breath and will continue to love her throughout her life. We welcome **(Groom)** into our family and pledge that we will be there to support them, but give them the independence they require in life. We love you.

Pastor: Who gives this man to be married to this woman?

Father of the Groom: Her father and mother who have loved him from his first breath and will continue to love him throughout his life. We welcome **(Bride)** into our family and pledge that we will be there to support them, but give them the independence they require in life. We love you.

Pastor to Couple: You are leaving your parents' homes to begin your own independent lives together, but you will also be establishing stronger emotional ties to each other. Friends and family are important in our lives, but turning to one another first in conversation, thoughts and relationship is vital. We need others to help us shape our lives and marriage, but they can only give us the love and enjoyment of their company to a point. Your loyalty now is to each other. Establishing that pattern is what a strong foundation means in marriage.

Pastor: Who gives this man and woman symbolically the right to develop a strong emotional tie to each other and growth in their marriage?

Best Man and Maid (Matron) of Honor (in unison): **(Bride)** and **(Groom)** on behalf of your friends. We will be in your lives to support you… laugh and cry with you… talk with you… counsel with you… listen to you… but never will we replace your spouse and your need to communicate with one another. We love you.

Pastor: There is a permanence in a strong home built upon a solid foundation. Together you will build a home through finances, jobs and physical belongings. Each of you will bring those items into this marriage. Never let them be obstructions to where you really want to be, but rather allow them to support your outlook of dreaming together, hoping together and setting goals together. Make them be building blocks to the future. A future that gives strength and energy to your marriage.

Groom: (Bride), my desire is that I be the man in your life who builds a strong and permanent home. I pledge to work at it daily!

Bride: (Groom), my desire is that I be the woman in your life who builds a strong and permanent home. I pledge to work at it daily!

Pastor: Intimacy in life is achievable, but does not come easily. There will be moments, we will not always be in sync, but those are the moments that we will ask, "What can I do for you?" "What are your needs?" Intimacy does not happen overnight, but will take a lifetime to achieve. Expect times of failure, but don't linger there, rather work continuously at making a strong marriage successful. Remember this is a journey… together.

Author Cheryl Roret wrote, "When each of you is giving 100% to the other, watch out! That is when rockets flare and love really blossoms!"

Pastor to Groom and **Bride:** Today, each of you has brought a ring as the symbol of your faithfulness and love in this marriage. The rings are built upon the concept of strength. The gold has been refined with fire and then shaped into a never ending circle. It represents the strength in your lives together knowing that there will be times that each of you goes through the fire either individually or as a couple. Let it give strength and not weakness in those moments.

Groom: I, **(Groom)**, give you, **(Bride)**, this ring as a symbol of my undying devotion and love to you.

Bride: (Groom), I happily accept this ring from you because I know it symbolizes your devotion and love to me now and forever.

Bride: I, **(Bride)**, give you, **(Groom)**, this ring as a symbol of my undying devotion and love to you.

Groom: (Bride), I happily accept this ring from you because I know it symbolizes your devotion and love to me now and forever.

Special Music: "May the Grace of Christ" by Stebbins

Pastoral Prayer for the Couple

Pastor to Groom: Do you, **(Groom)**, take this woman to be your lawfully wedded wife as long as you both shall live?

Groom: I do.

Pastor to Bride: Do you, **(Bride)**, take this man to be your lawfully wedded husband as long as you both shall live?

Bride: I do.

Pastor to Audience: This couple is pledging their love and devotion to each other now. Will you support them in this venture for a lifetime? If so, say, "We will."

Audience: "We will."

Pastor to Groom and Bride: You have exchanged rings, pledged your love and devotion to one another and given thought to a strong and successful marriage. Since you have enacted this, I declare you husband and wife by the authority of the **(Church)** and the state of **(State)**. What God has joined together let no one attempt to separate. **(Groom)**, you may now kiss your bride.

Ladies and gentlemen, it is my distinct honor to be the first to present to you Mr. and Mrs. **(Groom's First and Last Name)**.

Recessional: "When God Gave Me You" by Lillenas

CEREMONY 10
Gift of Love

Processional: "Melody of Love" by H. Engelmann

Pastor: Who gives this woman to be married to this man?

Father of the Bride: Her mother and I.

Pastor: Someone once said that love is a re-awakening of a relationship that teaches one how to relate to their spouse. In this new relationship you two are entering, you will achieve a greater oneness and deeper intimacy than you ever thought possible. God's Word will show you how to put each other first. That is His great gift to you… LOVE! The Scriptures help us find our way to love. 1 Corinthians 13:4 teaches us that love is patient and kind.

Listen to some other Scriptures that help define that style of love. (Best Man reads the Scriptures).

"Whoever is patient has great understanding…" (Proverbs 14:29 NIV)

"…Patience is better than pride." (Ecclesiastes 7:8 NIV)

"Be kind and compassionate to one another, forgiving each other, just as in Christ God forgave you." (Ephesians 4:32 NIV)

Groom to Bride (can be repeated after pastor or memorized): (Bride), I will love you and be there for you when your day is long and frustrating. I will share a smile when you need one. I will give you an encouraging word when the day has been negative. I will praise you for who you are. This is my pledge.

Bride to Groom (can be repeated after pastor or memorized): (Groom), I will love you and be there for you when your day is long and frustrating. I will share a smile when you need one. I will give you an encouraging word when the day has been negative. I will praise you for who you are. This is my pledge.

Pastor: Love is personal with truth at the heart of the matter. 1 Corinthians 13:6 states, "Love does not delight in evil, but rejoices with the truth." (NIV)
   Listen to some other Scriptures and thoughts that help define truth. (Mother of the groom reads the quotations).
   "…the truth shall set you free." (John 8:32b NIV)
   "Truth is the radiant manifestation of reality." (Simone Weil)
   "Truth and duty are always wedded. There is no duty which has not its corresponding truth." (Phillips Brooks)

Groom to Bride (can be repeated after pastor or memorized): (Bride), I will always be truthful to you. The truth opens my heart and makes it vulnerable to you. The truth challenges my mind to make me alert to you and your needs. The truth overcomes the fear that makes me a negative person to you and instead makes me positive focused on you. The truth makes me never wanting to be false to you, but always honest and forthright. To this end I, **(Bride)**, pledge you my love through truth.

Bride to Groom (can be repeated after pastor or memorized): (Groom), I will always be truthful to you. The truth opens my heart and makes it vulnerable to you. The truth challenges my mind to make me alert to you and your needs. The truth overcomes the fear that makes me a negative person to you and instead makes me positive focused on you. The truth makes me never wanting to be false to you, but always honest and forthright. To this end I, **(Groom)**, pledge you my love through truth.

Pastor: Love is persistent in its relationship. 1 Corinthians 13:8 says, "Love never fails. (NIV). That simply means it is persistent in all of genuine relationships. It never stops moving forward.

Hear the Word of the Lord and other thoughts about persistence. (Mother of the bride reads the quotations)
"Hatred stirs up dissension, but love covers over all wrongs." (Proverbs 10:12 NIV)
"I will search for the one my heart loves." (Song of Solomon 3:2 NIV)
"Never give up. Never give up." (Winston Churchill)

Groom to Bride (can be repeated after pastor or memorized): (Bride), I will be persistent in my love throughout our lives together. Our love will prevail through hardships, heartaches, handicaps, happiness, and health by helping us have the habit of hope. I, **(Groom)**, pledge you my persistent hope in our loving relationship.

Bride to Groom (can be repeated after pastor or memorized): (Groom), I will be persistent in my love throughout our lives together. Our love will prevail through hardships, heartaches, handicaps, happiness, and health by helping us have the habit of hope. I, **(Bride)**, pledge you my persistent hope in our loving relationship.

Pastor: What do you give as a symbol of your love?
Bride/Groom: We give rings as our symbol of love to one another. (Bride and Groom slip the rings on each other's fingers).

Pastor to Groom: Please repeat after me. I, **(Groom)**, take you, **(Bride)**, to be my wife to spend the rest of my life discovering more about you. I will endeavor to make your life fulfilled and satisfied daily.

Pastor to Bride: Please repeat after me. I, **(Bride)**, take you, **(Groom)** to be my husband to spend the rest of my life discovering more about you. I will endeavor to make your life fulfilled and satisfied daily.

Special Music: "I Will Be Here" (Christian World, Oklahoma City, Oklahoma, 1990).

Pastoral Prayer: Our loving God, **(Bride)** and **(Groom)** have discovered each other. They have dedicated themselves today to one another and to you. As they unite in marriage on this very important day, may you grant them your holy blessing upon them? Allow them now to discover the delicate balance in life of loving you and loving each other. May you ordain this marriage with your holy and divine presence. Never leave them… never forsake them… always provide your Holy Spirit to them. In the name of the Father, Son and Holy Spirit. Amen.

Pastor's Pronouncement:
Since **(Groom)** and **(Bride)** have discovered love in each other, let nothing or no one disrupt that love forever. You two have pledged your love to one another, exchanged rings with each other, and professed a desire to always be together as husband and wife. To that end, I pronounce you husband and wife by the authority of the State of **(State)** and the church of **(Church)**.
(Groom), you may now kiss your bride!

Pastor: Dear family and friends, it is my honor to present for the first time Mr. and Mrs. **(Groom's First and Last Name)**! What God has joined together let us rejoice and be glad therein!

Recessional: "Marche" by Charles Gounod

CEREMONY 11
Love Again

Processional: "If With All Your Heart" by Mendelssohn

Pastor: The writer of Genesis quotes God as saying about Adam, "It is not good that man should be alone; I will make a helpmeet for him" (Genesis 2:18 KJV). From the beginning of our recorded time, man and woman have shared life together as companions. **(Groom)** and **(Bride)** have come to this place because of free will. They have chosen each other and look forward to a lifetime together as companions helping one another along life's journey. They have prayed and sought God's will in this important matter of the heart. They desire to be together each is the completion of their life in the other.

The two of you have fulfillment in life, especially with children and grandchildren, but you still have a life ahead, filled with the gift of time and expressed in joy, hope and love. Someone said that the fervor of youth wanes, but the delight of age remains. Love keeps us young, innocent and beautiful.

We gather to celebrate what God has placed in your hearts, **(Groom)** and **(Bride)** , and to witness your coming together as husband and wife. Make your home a haven of peace to each other. Dedicate yourselves to bringing love to anyone fortunate enough to enter the doors of your home.

If there is anyone who would object to this marriage, let them speak now or remain silent forever.

Pastor: We now come to the moment of exchanging vows with one another. **(Groom)** and **(Bride)** , please join hands and look deeply into one another's eyes and hearts as you repeat your vows.

Pastor to Groom (Groom Repeats Vows): I, **(Groom)**, take you, **(Bride)**, into my heart for all the days of our lives. I promise to love you and share with you as my lawfully wedded wife. I promise to make you happy and share God's blessings with you. My desire to marry you is simple… I enjoy loving you!

Pastor to Bride (Bride Repeats Vows): I, **(Bride)**, take you, **(Groom)**, into my heart for all the days of our lives. I promise to love you and share with you as my lawfully wedded husband. I promise to make you happy and share God's blessings with you. My desire to marry you is simple… I enjoy loving you!

Pastoral Prayer of Thanksgiving: Our God, **(Groom)** and **(Bride)** have discovered the highest calling in life… loving someone other than themselves. As they unite in this life, help them to further the purpose You have called them into as husband and wife with an intense dedication to serving each other and You!

Each brings unique gifts and talents to this marriage that will be given to the other partner. In all their decisions may they use each other's gifts and talents to make good and solid decisions that will help resolve any problems. Through all sorrows and all joys may they be a support to one another. Today they start a life with love---a love that you have blessed and ordained. Let your blessing rest upon them constantly. In the name of the Father, Son, and Holy Spirit. Amen.

Pastor: Do each of you bring a ring to symbolize your love for one another?

Bride and Groom: Yes

Pastor to Groom: (Groom), please place on **(Bride)** finger the ring you give symbolizing your devotion to her. Repeat after me:

Groom Repeats: (Bride), I give you this ring as a symbol of my devoted love. It is a symbol to all of my loyalty and love. May our Heavenly Father bless our union together.

Pastor to Bride: (Bride), please repeat after me your words of acceptance.

Bride Repeats: (Groom), I accept your ring and will wear it as a symbol of my loyalty and love. I look forward to our Heavenly Father's blessing of our union together.

Pastor to Bride: (Bride), please place on **(Groom)** finger the ring you give symbolizing your devotion to him. Repeat after me:

Bride Repeats: (Groom), I give you this ring as a symbol of my devoted love. It is a symbol to all of my loyalty and love. May our Heavenly Father bless this union together.

Pastor to Groom: (Groom), please repeat after me your words of acceptance.

Groom Repeats: (Bride), I accept your ring and will wear it as a symbol of my loyalty and love. I look forward to our Heavenly Father's blessing of our union together.

Pronouncement by Pastor: (Groom) and **(Bride)**, you have discovered each other in your mature years of life. You will teach each other new things in this marriage as two separate and unique individuals. You see the miracle in one another that is invisible to others. YOU are the miracle for each other. Nurture that miracle in love. May this miracle of love never fade, but only sparkle brighter in the years ahead.

Now that you have pledged your love and faithfulness to each other. I take great pleasure in pronouncing you husband and wife by God's investment, the church's blessing, and the state's authorization.

Pastor to Groom: You may now kiss your bride.

Prayer of Blessing by Pastor:
O God who creates love, we come to you asking a blessing upon this couple. They have joined their hearts, their voices, their love together today signifying their desire to be husband and wife. We have been privileged to celebrate this joyous occasion with our friends, **(Groom)** and **(Bride)**. Let each day of their lives be filled to overflowing with love and excitement. Give them joy in the simple moments spent together with music, conversation around the kitchen table, walking the streets of their community, looking at photographs together, holding hands, giving thanks for each other, and attending your house of worship. Bless their children and grandchildren that they may find happiness in the new relationship that comes to them in their parents' happiness. We rejoice in this day of celebration!

Special Music: "God-Given Love" by Hawkins

Pastor: Ladies and Gentlemen may I introduce to you Mr. and Mrs. **(Groom's First and Last Name)**.

Recessional: "Love Theme from Romeo and Juliet" by Nino Rota

CEREMONY 12
Renewing the Vows of Love

This ceremony can be adapted for special years of renewal.

Processional: "Largo" (Xerxes) by Handel

Pastor to Congregation: Family and Friends of **(Groom)** and **(Bride)**, we have gathered here to witness the renewal of their wedding vows that were taken _____ years ago so they are celebrating their _____ anniversary. This celebration is truly a celebration of God who has brought these two together _____ years ago. At that time, these two wonderful individuals pledged their undying and unswerving devotion to one another in a display of mutual support and caring companionship. That day so many years ago contained pledges, commitments, blessings, along with hopes and dreams for the future. Their journey has brought them to this moment in time for a renewal and refreshing of those vows. We who have gathered today see in them the uniqueness of personalities and humanness. They bring a flavor of hope to each of us witnessing this today. They have found favor with God and with one another that we want to emulate through our marriage journeys.

Today's renewal is a public example and witness of God's faithfulness and commitment to **(Groom)** and **(Bride)**. Together **(Groom)** and **(Bride)** want to declare their continued commitment to the God who demonstrated and brought them to understanding love in human and divine ways.

Couple in Unison: Today, we come to reaffirm the covenant we first made before God. We will continue to spend the rest of our days in a loving, sharing and caring relationship with each other. We renew our support of each other. We will continue to affirm in positive ways one another. He demonstrated to us how to love by sacrificially giving of life through his death and resurrection. We reaffirm our faith in our God as well as one another.

Scripture Reading by Family Member: 1 Corinthians 13

Pastor: The hallmarks of your lives have been fairness, faithfulness, and fellowship toward one another. The renewal of your vows will bear the marks that have established you and carried you all of these years.

Husband: Today, my loving wife,**(Bride)**, I renew my vows to you.

(Bride), I love you now more than I loved you at the beginning of our marriage. Life's experiences have forged us together in ways we never dreamed possible from the start. You have demonstrated genuine love to me and I revel in it. It has become my source of hope, rejoicing and fulfillment. You have always been sensitive to God's love as He has given you wisdom through His Spirit. Our children (and grandchildren) rise to call you blessed for you are truly a woman of love and I celebrate you and renew my commitment to you for the rest of my life. How blessed I am!

Wife: Today, my loving husband, **(Groom)**, I renew my vows to you.

(Groom), I love you, too, now more than I loved you at the beginning of our marriage. Life's experiences have forged us together in ways we never dreamed possible from the start. You have demonstrated genuine love and leadership in our marriage and I thank God for it. It has become my source of hope, rejoicing and fulfillment. You have always been sensitive to God's love as He has given you wisdom through His Spirit. Our children (grandchildren) rise to thank you for your constant care for me. Today, I celebrate you and renew my commitment to you for the rest of my life. How blessed I am!

Scripture Reading: Colossians 3:12-14 (Read by a family member).

Prayer: A prayer from one of the family members on behalf of family and friends for the example of this couple's love.

Pastor: We celebrate this sacred time and the renewal of the vows of **(Groom)** and **(Bride)** today! As a minister of the Lord, I pronounce that with renewed faith, love, commitment and resolve, they are husband and wife.
You may kiss your wife.

Benediction of Peace: "The peace of God, which transcends all understanding,… guard your hearts and minds in Christ Jesus" (Phil. 4:7). AMEN.

MUSIC SUGGESTIONS FOR WEDDINGS

Processionals

"Agnus Dei" by Georges Bizet
"Come Ye Blessed" by John P. Scott
"He Shall Feed His Flock" by Handel
"Hail Thee, Festival Day" by Ralph Vaughn Williams
"If With All Your Hearts" by Mendelssohn
"Largo (Xerxes)" by Handel
"Melody of Love" by H. Engelmann
"Panis Angelicus" by Franck
"Jesu, Joy of Man's Desiring" by Bach
"Sanctus" (St. Ceiclia) by Gounod
"Bridal Chorus" (Lohengrin) by Wagner
"Love Theme from Romeo and Juliet" by Nino Rota

Vocals Or Instrumentals

"Andante Cantabile" by William Stickles
"A Time for Us" by Larry Kusik and Eddie Snyder
"Because" by D'Hardelot
"Come Live Your Love With Me" by Nino Rota, Larry Kusik, and Billy Meshel
"Entreat Me Not to Leave Thee" by Charles Gounod
"From This Day Forth" by Hawkins
"God-given Love" by Hawkins
"Hooray for Love" by Leo Robin and Harold Arlen
"I Come to Thee" by Beatrice Fenner and Adaptation by Chester Nordman
"I Concentrate on You" by Cole Porter
"I Do" by Jos.Cassin
"I Love You Truly" by Bond
"I Take Thee, Dear" by Lucile Johnson and Ray Carter

"Liebestraum" by Franz Liszt
"Love Story" by Carl Sigman and Francis Lai
"Lover" by Lorenz Hart and Richard Rodgers
"May the Grace of Christ" by Stebbins
"My Heart Ever Faithful" by Johann Sebastian Bach
"O God of Love" by Niccum
"O God, Our Help in Ages Past" by Croft
"O Love Divine and Golden" by Dykes
"O Perfect Love" by Barnby
"O Promise Me" by DeKoven
"Romance" by Anton Rubinstein
"Saviour, Like a Shepherd Lead Us" by Bradbury
"So Love I Thee" by Grieg
"Speak Softly Love" by Larry Kusik
"Take our Lives" by Malan
"The Lord's Prayer" by Felix Mendelssohn
"Walk Hand and Hand" by Johnny Cowell
"Wedding Prayer" by M. J. Crowder

Recessionals

"When God Gave Me You" by Lillenas
"Guide Me, O Thou Great Jehovah" by Hughes
"How Firm a Foundation" Early American
"Marche" by Charles Gounod
"Moonlight Sonata" by Ludwig van Beethovan
"Non Nobis, Domine" from Henry V by Patrick Doyle
"Recessional" by William Sticlkes
"Trumpet Air" by Purcell
"Wedding March" by Mendelssohn
"Traumerei" by Robert Schumann

SUGGESTED SCRIPTURES

Use the best translation that fits the occasion for your reading.

Genesis 1:27-28	Matthew 25:34-36
Genesis 2:7	John 8:32b
Genesis 2:15-16	John 13:34-35
Genesis 2:18-24	John 15:12
Genesis 29:18	Romans 15:4-6
Numbers 6:24-26	I Corinthians 7:4
Psalm 103:17-18	I Corinthians 13:1-13
Proverbs 3:1-6	II Corinthians 13:14
Proverbs 14:29	Galatians 4:1-3
Proverbs 18:22	Ephesians 4:4-7a
Proverbs 20:28	Ephesians 5:1
Proverbs 21:21	Ephesians 5:21-28
Ecclesiastes 4:9	Philippians 4:7
Ecclesiastes 7:8	Colossians 3:12-14
Song of Songs 3:2	Colossians 3:15-17
Song of Songs 8:7	Hebrews 13:4
Matthew 5:13-16	James 1:19-20
Matthew 6:33	I John 3:18
Matthew 19:4-6	Revelation 22:17

Wedding Sermons

by Randall Hartman

1 Peter 4:8-11a

Love's Got You Covered

> *Above all, love each other deeply, because love covers over a multitude of sins. Offer hospitality to one another without grumbling. Each of you should use whatever gift you have received to serve others, as faithful stewards of God's grace in its various forms. If anyone speaks, they should do so as one who speaks the very words of God.* — 1 Peter 4:8-11a

On this happy day, your love for each other is center stage.

In the days ahead, you will face both good and bad days. The married couples attending today, will affirm that there will be days when you will need to work on your marriage. But that's okay. Your love for each other has got you covered.

Even with the best of intentions, there will be times when you will disappoint or fail your spouse. Verse 8 reminds us that love covers a multitude of sins. Love is so powerful it refuses to cling to any marriage mistakes. Your love for each other will rise above any future sorrows or failures.

Your love for each other, which we celebrate today, has you covered.

First, as a married couple, you are covered in the area of what you think. The text points out we should offer hospitality without grumbling. Grumbling is an outward expression of what we think. A strong love for each other ought to guide how you think.

In every situation, give each other the benefit of the doubt. Assume the best. Think about the positive far more than the negative.

Regarding what you think, love's got you covered.

Second, as a married couple, you are covered in the area of what you do. Verse 10 begins like this: "Each of you should use whatever gift you have received to serve others…" Love is best viewed as a verb instead of a noun. Love is action, not emotion.

In your marriage, allow your love for each other to spur you to do good things. If you listen to your heart, your actions will help your marriage, not hurt it.

Regarding what you do, love's got you covered.

Third, you are covered in the area of what you say. Verse 11 proclaims: "If anyone speaks, they should do so as one who speaks the very words of God." Words wound or heal. Words bring hope or despair. In a marriage the use of words is important.

But as time passes, you will face the temptation to become careless with your words. Strive to not give in to that temptation. Careless words are often hurting words.

Regarding what you say, love's got you covered.

Love really does win the day. With each passing day, your strong love for each other will grow. And as it grows it will protect your marriage. In the good times and the challenging times, it's good to know, love's got you covered.

Matthew 6:21-23

Looking Good!

> *For where your treasure is, there your heart will be also. The eye is the lamp of the body. If your eyes are good, your whole body will be full of light. But if your eyes are bad, your whole body will be full of darkness. If then the light within you is darkness, how great is that darkness!* — Matthew 6:21-23

We tend to focus on what we love. Jesus said it like this, "For where your treasure is, there your heart will be also."

The entrepreneur focuses on her business.

The miser focuses on his pennies.

The activist focuses on his cause.

But on this day, we focus on you. Friends and family are here because they love you. You have our attention. All eyes are on you.

And because of your love for each other, your attention is focused on the one standing next to you. In this moment, you see each other in a positive light.

Have you ever noticed how two different people can look at the same thing and yet see it differently? Any policeman can affirm this truth. As he gathers accident reports from witnesses, he's not surprised when details vary. It isn't that people are lying. It's that people have a different way of looking at the same facts.

Some people have a negative eye; others a positive eye. For example, one person might view a pay raise with gratitude and yet another might be upset it wasn't more money.

How you see, determines what you see.

In this moment you stand before these witnesses and look at each other. You see the love of your life ready to exchange vows with you. Life is filled with promise. Things are looking good.

I challenge both of you to always look at each other in a positive light. Too many marriages started out with a positive view of each other but that changes. Troubles came and they focused on the negative. Their good vision turned bad.

If your view of your spouse starts to go dark, there's a problem. Verse 23 reminds us, "if your eyes are bad, your whole body will be full of darkness." This is where a marriage starts to fall apart. It begins when we no longer view our loved one in a positive light.

The challenge of married life is to look at each other everyday in the best light. Choose to see the positive over the negative. This is a choice you must make if your marriage is to thrive.

Every couple must face the reality of being married to an imperfect person. The negatives will crop up. But don't dwell on those things. Force yourself to dwell on the positives. Never give in to the temptation to view your spouse in a less than positive light.

My prayer for you is that on your fiftieth wedding anniversary, you will look at each other with a twinkle in your eye. And, after all those years, what you see is still looking good.

John 15:12-13

No Plan B

"My command is this: Love each other as I have loved you. Greater love has no one than this, that he lay down his life for his friends." — John 15:12-13

Jesus shares these words with his friends. He knows the Garden of Gethsemane arrest is happening soon and would result in crucifixion. But He never backed down. Deep love makes no plans for failure.

Today we celebrate the great love you have for each other. It is a love based on a deep friendship. No doubt you remember the first time you laid eyes on each other. Then, with the passing of time, you became friends. That friendship turned into a deep love. And now we are here to solemnize your love by exchanging marriage vows.

Have you ever wondered why the typical wedding ceremony includes these words: "for better, for worse, in sickness and in health?" It's because experience teaches us that all marriages will face challenges. And too often, when those challenges arise, the marriage falls apart.

On this beautiful day filled with excitement and joy, it's difficult to imagine. But every marriage will face difficult days.

These words from Jesus to His friends remind us of two important truths as you prepare for life together.

The first truth is this: real love is not based on emotion but on an act of the will.

Do you find it odd that Jesus uses the word "command" in the context of love? And then He follows with the words, "Love each other…" When you face difficult times, never forget the vows you take today. Remember the commitment you made here in front of these witnesses. Exercise your ability to choose and keep on loving your spouse regardless of the circumstances.

The second truth is this: real love is demonstrated by full sacrifice to your spouse.

In too many marriages the partners become more focused on themselves than on their spouse. Instead of "us" it becomes "me." And if you are not careful, a rift will form. But Jesus models for us the fact that a deep love is all about sacrifice and surrender to the other person. He proved it when He went to the cross. Your marriage will survive anything if you look out for the interests of your spouse before your own.

In our culture too many marriages crash upon the rocks of heartache and disappointment. But your marriage will last if you remember, there is no Plan B.

In the sixteenth century, Captain Cortez landed with his men in Veracruz. His men knew they faced many dangers, including battle with the Incas. He became aware of talk among the men of returning to their homeland. Cortez destroyed the boats. He got his message across: there is no Plan B. Their only recourse was to fight hard for victory.

As you prepare to exchange your vows, remind yourself this is for life. Plan on loving each other as you journey through life together. Like every marriage you will face challenges. But your marriage will survive and thrive because there is no Plan B.

Hear the words of Jesus one more time and allow them to be your commitment to each other.

"My command is this: Love each other as I have loved you. Greater love has no one than this, that he lay down his life for his friends."

Joshua 24:14-15

Getting Off On The Right Start

> *"Now fear the Lord and serve him with all faithfulness. Throw away the gods your forefathers worshiped beyond the River and in Egypt, and serve the Lord. But if serving the Lord seems undesirable to you, then choose for yourselves this day whom you will serve, whether the gods your forefathers served beyond the River, or the gods of the Amorites, in whose land you are living. But as for me and my household, we will serve the Lord."* — Joshua 24:14-15

In everything you do, it's important to get off on the right start. That's true in releasing the hunting arrow aimed at a deer or releasing a bowling ball aimed at the pins. But it's especially true in marriage. It's vital to get off on the right start.

On this day, you enter into a great journey together. At the end of this ceremony the two of you will become one. You will say goodbye to family and friends, put away the fancy clothes, and climb into your car. Life together is only hours away.

But it's important to start out right. Like bowling and hunting, marriage is so much easier if you get it right from the beginning.

How do you start out right? The answer is found in the Old Testament story of Joshua and the renewal of the covenant. The word covenant ought to be familiar to you. It is what you are doing here today. It is the making of an agreement between two parties. And a major part of any covenant is a focus on a list of agreed duties of both parties.

At the start of verse 24, Joshua reminds the people of the importance of their allegiance to God. In the context of the covenant, God calls upon them to serve only him. It is a decision they need to make. If they agree, then they are off on the right start. If they fail to agree, then they will head down a road of sorrow and hurt.

Joshua wants the people to know he has made the decision to put God first in his own family. He leads by example. And now, 3,000 years later he still sets the example for young couples to follow.

Heeding this call to serve only God, is the way to get your marriage off on the right start. As you make your covenant to each other, please consider this challenge: "choose for yourselves this day whom you will serve."

We all know of couples who have made the wrong choice. They decided to ignore the solid advice of Joshua. They completed the wedding ceremony, headed out on life's road, and left God behind. No wonder they encountered heartache.

This is the day you enter into a covenant with each other. But it is also the day you must pay attention to the challenge of Joshua: "choose for yourselves this day whom you serve." Consider with care those words. Get your marriage off to the right start. Decide to put God first in your marriage.

May your covenant with each other be strengthened by your determination to make God the center of your home!

Genesis. 2:18-25

Better Together

The Lord God said, "It is not good for the man to be alone. I will make a helper suitable for him."

Now the Lord God had formed out of the ground all the wild animals and all the birds in the sky. He brought them to the man to see what he would name them; and whatever the man called each living creature, that was its name. So the man gave names to all the livestock, the birds in the sky and all the wild animals.

But for Adam no suitable helper was found.[1] So the Lord God caused the man to fall into a deep sleep; and while he was sleeping, he took one of the man's ribs and then closed up the place with flesh. Then the Lord God made a woman from the rib he had taken out of the man, and he brought her to the man.

The man said, "This is now bone of my bones and flesh of my flesh; she shall be called 'woman,' for she was taken out of man."

That is why a man leaves his father and mother and is united to his wife, and they become one flesh. Adam and his wife were both naked, and they felt no shame. — Genesis 2:18-25

Have you ever noticed the Bible is filled with humor? For example, one of the funniest verses is found in Genesis 2:20: "So the man gave names to all the livestock, the birds in the sky and all the wild animals. But for Adam no suitable helper was found."

Do you see the humor?

The first part of the verse, reveals that Adam named the livestock, birds, and wild animals. The next part of the phrase says, "But for Adam no suitable helper was found."

At first glance these two sentences appear unrelated. What could be connection between Adam naming the animals and the observation he needed a helper?

It's obvious. Adam could've used help in naming the animals. And if you think this is far fetched, remind yourself of a few animal names he chose: hippopotamus and platypus. God realized Adam needed a helper!

In the next verse, God creates a woman out of Adam's rib. Adam now has his helper. He will no longer need to go through life alone. And if he ever gets another opportunity to name more animals, Eve is there to help him get it right.

This ancient text reminds us that a man and woman are better together. A man is incomplete without a woman. A woman is incomplete without a man. In marriage there is a teaming up of resources. Each person in the marriage brings their own strengths and weaknesses. But when the two are brought together, there is a unified strength. You are better together.

This means in your marriage, you ought to look for the ways you complement each other. Marriage isn't about picking at each others' weaknesses. Instead, it's about embracing the strengths of each partner so you can navigate the journey ahead with a greater chance of success.

In verse 24, the writer observes that in marriage a man and woman leave their parents and become one. This makes sense. The woman, who was made out of the man's rib, is joined with the man. They complete each other. They belong together. They are better together.

Today, the two of you will become one. This means shifting your priority from your parents to your spouse. They will always remain loved and valued. But from this day forward, God intends for your top priority to be each other.

As you focus on each other, strive to discover the ways you complement each other. Each of you will be better at some aspects of marriage than the other. Don't see this as competition but as an opportunity to complement each other.

As the years roll by, you will discover you really are better together!

Colossians 3:14-17

Dress For Marriage Success

And over all these virtues put on love, which binds them all together in perfect unity.
Let the peace of Christ rule in your hearts, since as members of one body you were called to peace. And be thankful. Let the word of Christ dwell in you richly as you teach and admonish one another with all wisdom, and as you sing psalms, hymns and spiritual songs with gratitude in your hearts to God. And whatever you do, whether in word or deed, do it all in the name of the Lord Jesus, giving thanks to God the Father through him. — Colossians 3:14-17

It's evident great care has gone into this day. We look around and smile with appreciation at the beauty around us. This is especially true of the radiant bride and groom. They've chosen what to wear this day with considerable deliberation.

Years ago, a bride would assemble with care more than her wedding dress. She would spend months accumulating her clothes for the start of her married life. The custom recognizes that it's one thing to look nice for the wedding, but it's also important to plan for the days after the wedding. The word for these starting-out clothes is "trousseau."

The Apostle Paul writes to the people in the church at Colosse. As he writes he instructs them regarding the importance of putting on certain virtues. Those verses provide a picture of a trousseau which husband and wife ought to put on to assure a successful marriage.

There are four pieces of clothing you need to put on each morning of your married lives.

Put on love. Love is the belt which pulls everything together. Without the belt of love everything else falls apart. Begin each morning of your married life reminding yourself of your deep love for your spouse. Allow your love to pull you tighter to one another.

Put on peace. In this context the word peace means the absence of mental stress or anxiety. Each of you must work at the task of making your home a place of peace. Allow it to be a sanctuary from the cares of life.

Put on wisdom. There will be times emotions will try to take you down a wrong road. Don't let that happen. Instead of lashing out, put on wisdom. Allow clear thinking to rule the day. Make decisions based on facts and not out of control emotions.

Put on thankfulness. This word from verse 17 is the word from which we get "eucharist." It's the deep thanks we have for what Christ has done for us in His sacrificial death. This is the kind of thankfulness you need to have for your spouse. Give thanks every day for your spouse and the sacrifices being made for you.

This is your trousseau of virtues you must have when heading into married life. Each one is important. Together they form a complete outfit which will serve you well in the years ahead.

Don't miss the key component of this trousseau. The phrase "put on" means you must decide and act. It's not enough to gather these virtues, but you must decide to put them on. This is not about looking good but about being good. Every morning, as you face another day together, put on love, peace, wisdom, and thankfulness.

You have dressed for a terrific wedding. And now you have assembled a wardrobe of virtues for your life together. Make the decision that every day of your married life you will dress for success!

Song of Songs 2:8-13

Off On An Adventure

Listen! My beloved! Look! Here he comes, leaping across the mountains, bounding over the hills. My beloved is like a gazelle or a young stag. Look! There he stands behind our wall, gazing through the windows, peering through the lattice. My beloved spoke and said to me, "Arise, my darling, my beautiful one, come with me. See! The winter is past; the rains are over and gone."Flowers appear on the earth; the season of singing has come, the cooing of doves is heard in our land. The fig tree forms its early fruit; the blossoming vines spread their fragrance. Arise, come, my darling; my beautiful one, come with me." — Song of Songs 2:8-13

The Bible book known as the Song of Songs confounds ancient and contemporary readers. The words found in the text resonate with joy, wonder, and physical excitement. Readers often think, "Surely there is a deeper meaning to these chapters?"

Perhaps rich layers of meaning hide under the surface of the plain words. But I favor giving these verses a chance to speak in their simplest form. And as we allow the text to speak for itself, it suggests that marriage is a wonderful adventure.

This verses portray the male lover as a deer bounding over the mountains seeking his love. He's playful, eager, and ready to sweep up his bride. The timing is right: flowers have bloomed, the birds sing, and the fruit appears on the trees and vines. Now, is the time for adventure.

Now is the time for you. The timing is right. You've made plans and we see the results of those plans all around us. This is your moment. You stand side by side with the one you've chosen to travel through life.

In minutes, this service will conclude. You will strike out on your big adventure.

But as the days turn into weeks, and the weeks months, you must never forget that adventures include challenge and struggle. By definition, adventure means an undertaking often involving danger and unknown risks. Marriage is an adventure in every sense of the word.

Think of the great adventures recorded in history.

In 1803 Lewis and Clark headed west to find a way to the Pacific Ocean. Battling a long list of hardships, they reached their goal. Their adventure was not for the weak-hearted.

In 1953 Edmund Hillary embraced the adventure of climbing Mt. Everest. In spite of the bitter cold and lack of oxygen at high altitudes, he became the first person to stand on the peak on May 29, 1953. Since then many have tried to replicate the feat. Only a few experienced success.

And if history isn't your thing, remind yourself that Dorothy made it back to Kansas by following the yellow brick road and battling witches and flying monkeys. Lions, and tigers, and bears "O my!"

What keeps you going on this great adventure when adversity comes? It is the memory of this moment. When the bottom falls out or the trail becomes rocky, remember this perfect day. Don't forget the vows you've exchanged. Embrace the happiness of this day when sorrow comes. Look deep into the eyes of your loved one and burn the image into your consciousness.

You are off on a great adventure called marriage. No one doubts challenges are ahead. But you have this moment. Never forget this day. Cross the finish line side by side.

Deuteronomy 11:10-15

A New Land Awaits!

The land you are entering to take over is not like the land of Egypt, from which you have come, where you planted your seed and irrigated it by foot as in a vegetable garden. ¹But the land you are crossing the Jordan to take possession of is a land of mountains and valleys that drinks rain from heaven. It is a land the Lord your God cares for; the eyes of the Lord your God are continually on it from the beginning of the year to its end.

So if you faithfully obey the commands I am giving you today — to love the Lord your God and to serve him with all your heart and with all your soul — then I will send rain on your land in its season, both autumn and spring rains, so that you may gather in your grain, new wine and oil. I will provide grass in the fields for your cattle, and you will eat and be satisfied. — Deuteronomy 11:10-15

The people of God stood on the banks of the Jordan River with joyful anticipation. Egypt was far behind them. The problems of the wilderness wanderings were now memories. Before them lay the land God had promised his people many years early. It was a land prepared for them by God. Soon they would know the joy of living in the Promised Land.

These verses record part of the actual covenant, or agreement, God made with His people. In verses 13-14 we see that if they obey and love God, then an awesome future is ahead. But it all depends on keeping God in the middle of the relationship.

History tells us God's people rebelled against him many times. They shoved Him out of the picture and did things their way. It's no wonder they experienced so much heartache.

These verses suggest a couple of truths about your marriage.

First, it's appropriate to think of your marriage as a place God created for you a long time ago. Like the Israelites of long ago, you stand on the edge of the Jordan River, ready to cross over into new territory.

Before you were born, God looked out across the eons and knew the two of you would fall in love. He brought you together. It is through His guiding hand that the two of you stand on the verge of entering into the land of holy matrimony.

Second, like the people of God, you must keep Him in the center of your relationship.

This is not a suggestion for a good marriage. It is the only way for your marriage to be like living in the Promised Land. It all hinges on whether or not you keep God at the core of your marriage.

This is why things fell apart in the Garden of Eden. God created a stunning place and put the first couple in the middle of it. But there was one catch: don't eat from the tree of life. When Adam and Eve disobeyed God they lost the garden. They failed to keep God in the center of the relationship.

There may be a few witnesses hearing these words who are thinking, "My marriage isn't like living in the Garden of Eden!" It's true. Not many marriages are like that. And the reason for this is that too many marriages fail to keep God at the center of their relationship.

This might sound far-fetched until you realize that marriage is a covenant. It is a covenant in the same way that the people of God made a covenant with Him.

Your marriage can be different. It can be one of those rare marriages that resembles living in the Garden of Eden.

1 Corinthians 13:4-7

The Magical Power Of Love

> *Love is patient, love is kind. It does not envy, it does not boast, it is not proud. It does not dishonor others, it is not self-seeking, it is not easily angered, it keeps no record of wrongs. Love does not delight in evil but rejoices with the truth. It always protects, always trusts, always hopes, always perseveres.* — 1 Corinthians 13:4-7

This day is all about love! Love prompts us to change our schedules and bring us together. Love turns the night to day. Love brings hope to the hopeless. Love captures the attention of every poet and dreamer. There is magical power in love.

But what does it mean to say, "I love you?" The meaning of the word "love" is a slippery thing. We say, "I love football" or "I love peanut butter and mayonnaise sandwiches."

The Bible, however, is more careful in the use of the word love. There are three different words from the original language which we translate as love.

The first is the word from which we get the idea of brotherly love. It is the word built into Philadelphia, known as the "city of brotherly love."

The second is the word for love meaning physical attraction. It is the word from which we get the word erotic.

But the word Paul uses here for love is quite different. It is a word suggesting a love by choice.

This biblical idea of love stands in stark contrast to our contemporary view of love. We often hear people say, "I couldn't help myself. I just fell in love." This notion of love suggests that a mythical fairy came to life and sprinkled magical love dust in our face. We were, as the theory suggests, unable to do anything but love our spouse.

Do you see the dangerous conclusion of this popular view of love? If you fell into love, you can fall out of love. When you see love as something beyond your choice then it means you are unable to choose to remain in love. This view of love causes incredible heartache and leads down the path of divorce.

Groom and bride please don't stand here today thinking of love as an irresistible force. In these verses the Apostle Paul uses a word for love that embraces the idea of choice. You are here today exchanging vows. And you are not here because some sort of fairy dust clouded your otherwise good judgment. You are here, on the contrary, because you have chosen to be here. You chose to love each other. And you enter into this ceremony today because you want to love each other.

This means the way ahead for you is clear. In your marriage keep choosing to love. When the way becomes difficult, as it will, choose love. When the disappointments come and your imperfections pop to the surface, choose love. If life decides to throw tragedy into your path, choose love.

Real love, is far stronger than any magical fairy dust. In this moment you choose love. May this be your choice forever. And if you keep choosing love, your marriage will stretch on out into eternity. That's magical!

Matthew 19:4-6

One Plus One Equals One

> *"Haven't you read," he replied, "that at the beginning the Creator 'made them male and female,' and said, 'For this reason a man will leave his father and mother and be united to his wife, and the two will become one flesh'? So they are no longer two, but one flesh. Therefore what God has joined together, let no one separate." — Matthew 19:4-6*

I know you've heard of modern math. But have you heard of marriage math?

Marriage math is illustrated by a simple equation: one plus one equals one. At first glance this seems impossible. It defies logic. Our minds rebel against thinking that this equation can be true. It makes no sense.

Welcome to marriage. To be married, according to the words of Jesus, is to live in the land that defies logic. It is to embrace the crazy idea that one plus one equals one.

Jesus says it like this: "...they are no longer two, but one flesh." Before marriage, you are two distinct individuals. Each of you have your own checkbook, your own dreams, your own life goals. But in marriage the two become one. You join together and become a single entity.

This line of thinking troubles some people. They argue that marriage does not take the two and form one. And it's often true; not every married couple becomes one flesh. But those who fail to become one will find it difficult to keep their marriage intact. It's important for the two of you to become one flesh.

Those who shun this kind of thinking do so because they don't really understand the concept of marriage. To grasp this mysterious marriage math, think of the creation story.

In the early chapters of Genesis we see that man floundered by himself. God saw he needed a helper. The story reveals that God took a rib out of Adam's side and used it to create Eve. Do you catch the significance of this? One became two. Through the remainder of his life, the one God created for him, journeyed with Adam.

You two were made for each other. Until now you wandered through life alone. You were on separate paths. But in this marriage moment, the two of you will begin a life-journey of walking side by side.

It's important to realize that when Adam and Eve hooked up, each of them retained their own personhood. Adam didn't disappear. Eve remained Eve. But there was something different. Out of one, became two. But when traveled through life side by side they once again become one.

With each passing year, your marriage will grow. You will learn the joys of becoming one. And, at the same time, you will discover that the person you are now will become better and stronger by being together.

This is such an important truth Jesus makes it clear that becoming one is a permanent arrangement. From this day forward your highest priority is to each other. There is nothing and no one who should ever come between you.

May prayer for you is that in your marriage, you learn the joy of one plus one equals one.

Ecclesiastes 4:9-10

The Surprising Synergy Of Marriage

> *Two are better than one, because they have a good return for their labor:*
> *If either of them falls down, one can help the other up.*
> *But pity anyone who falls*
> *and has no one to help them up.* — Ecclesiastes 4:9-10

It is love which brings us together on this special day. As you think about this day, I'm confident the last thing on your mind are the laws of mathematics. But thinking about math reminds us of the uniqueness of marriage.

Teachers tell students math operates on unbreakable laws. But they ignore the power of love. Marriage is so powerful it even changes the laws of math.

Before a man and woman experience marriage the normal rules of math apply. One plus one is always two. But the act of marriage changes the laws of math forever. When a man and woman join together in holy matrimony, one plus one no longer equals two. Once the marriage takes place, one plus one equals three.

This is not a new concept. The word "synergy" captures the concept. Synergy is when two people work together to do more than they could on their own.

Think of two people working to landscape a yard. It's a mistake to assign one person the front yard and the back yard to the other worker. The better way is to let them work together. They will do more work and better work if they are a team. In this example, one plus one equals three.

This is how marriage works. Ecclesiastes 4:9 says, "Two are better than one, because they have a good return for their labor…"

Those words speak to what is happening here. Today, as you exchange vows and pledge your love to each other, you are about to change the laws of mathematics. As you journey through life together you will go farther and better than you would on your own.

From this day forward, your combined efforts in life will yield a greater life than if you lived alone. This means:

1. You need each other.

Often a preacher proclaims that through marriage the two will become one. That's true. But it is also true to say that the two will become three. As you join your lives together you will learn to rely upon each other. Why? Because one plus one is three.

2. You must each do your part.

This verse serves as a reminder that each of you has a part to play. A real marriage is about two people each giving the relationship their best efforts. There will be good days and a few bad days, but as you put forth your best effort, you will create a wonderful life.

3. Your marriage will thrive as you work together as a team.

Too many marriages fail because the partners insist on maintaining their individuality. Never fear. At the end of this ceremony, you will still be the person you are now. But you will know the joy of one plus one equaling three.

Ephesians 5:22-28

The Way It Works

Wives, submit yourselves to your own husbands as you do to the Lord. For the husband is the head of the wife as Christ is the head of the church, his body, of which he is the Savior. Now as the church submits to Christ, so also wives should submit to their husbands in everything.

Husbands, love your wives, just as Christ loved the church and gave himself up for her to make her holy, cleansing her by the washing with water through the word, and to present her to himself as a radiant church, without stain or wrinkle or any other blemish, but holy and blameless. In this same way, husbands ought to love their wives as their own bodies. He who loves his wife loves himself. — Ephesians 5:22-28

Many preachers avoid speaking on these verses. They recognize the obvious potential minefield of misunderstanding. And with good reason.

Readers often distort these verses into a perversion of the real meaning. Too many people point to this passage as a way to justify a husband who mistreats his wife. But, when understood, this passage represents a beautiful picture of the marriage relationship.

The great truth in this passage unlocks when we consider both parts together. One side of the relationship cannot be understood without the other.

Think of the opening phrase, "Wives, submit yourselves to your own husbands." If we stop there and place a period, we are asking for trouble! To expect a wife to be a doormat for her husband is to invite a union of heartache and misunderstanding.

But the passage goes on with a challenge for the husband. The instruction for the husband is to love their wife "just as Christ loved the church and gave himself up for her." In a flash the picture changes. How did Christ give Himself up for the church? He had such love that He died on the cross. He volunteered to die for His bride.

The husband is to love his wife with a sacrificial love. It is the kind of relationship where the husband would be willing to die for his mate. This means he puts her first. He stands up for her. He defends her. He is her champion in all things. His willingness to go to bat for her knows no bounds. Groom, this is the kind of love you are to have for bride.

This means you will not be a demanding and self-seeking husband. You are not entering into this relationship with a golden scepter with which to rule your wife. The opposite is true. Your love for your bride is so strong you will always put her first.

After embracing this truth, it is much easier to deal with the phrase, "Wives submit to your husband."

What wife wouldn't volunteer to do everything possible for a husband who would die for her? "Wives submit yourselves to your own husbands," takes on a different flavor when viewed in context. The submission of the wife rests on the fact she has a champion at her side.

This submission by the wife is not based on a legalistic and unbending rule. Not at all. It rests on an explosion of loving gratitude from the heart of a wife who knows what it means to experience a deep love.

Your future is bright. The truth of this passage will become even clearer as you wade into the deep end of the pool called love. This is the way marriage works!

www.ingramcontent.com/pod-product-compliance
Lightning Source LLC
Chambersburg PA
CBHW021018090426
42738CB00007B/818